# Extremely WEIRD FISHES

## Text by Sarah Lovett

**John Muir Publications**
**Santa Fe, New Mexico**

**Very Special Thanks to**
**William L. Gannon,** Museum of Southwestern Biology, University of New Mexico
**Dr. Manuel C. Molles,** Department of Biology, University of New Mexico
**Charles Kelty,** Petpourri, Santa Fe, New Mexico
**Peter Sanders,** Pete's Pets, Santa Fe, New Mexico

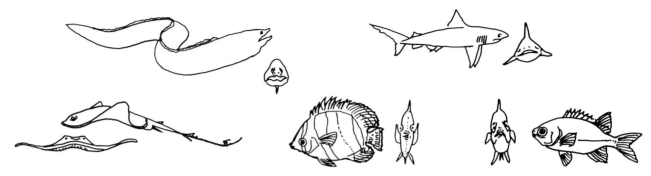

John Muir Publications, P.O. Box 613, Santa Fe, New Mexico 87504

© 1992 by John Muir Publications

First edition. Fourth printing September 1994

Library of Congress Cataloging-in-Publication Data
Lovett, Sarah, 1953-
     Extremely weird fishes / text by Sarah Lovett ; [illustrations,
Mary Sundstrom, Mary Lambert]. — 1st ed.
     p.  cm.
     Includes index.
     ISBN 1-56261-041-4
     1. Rare fishes—Juvenile literature. 2. Fishes—Juvenile
literature. I. Sundstrom, Mary. II. Lambert, Mary. III. Title.
QL617.2.L68   1992
597—dc20

92-7663
CIP
AC

Extremely Weird Logo Art: Peter Aschwanden
Illustrations: Mary Sundstrom, Mary Lambert
Design: Sally Blakemore
Typography: Copygraphics, Inc., Santa Fe, New Mexico
Printer: Inland Press

Distributed to the book trade by
W. W. Norton & Co., Inc.
New York, New York

Distributed to the education market by
Wright Group Publishing, Inc.
19201 120th Avenue N.E.
Bothell, Washington 98011-9512

Each fish's body can be classified by shape. For instance, a shark's body is *fusiform*, or topedo-shaped, for swift swimming. The angelfish is *laterally flattened*, which means it is thin as a pancake side to side (the easier to slip between the cracks). As a means of locomotion, rays and skates are flattened top to bottom, or *dorsoventrally compressed*. The American eel is *attenuated*—long and narrow—and able to live in small rocky caves. Many fishes are combination shapes.

Cover photo: Frogfish (Family: *Antenariidae*)
Frogfishes live close to coral reefs in warm seas around the world. Their balloon-shaped, bumpy, knobby bodies provide camouflage so they can surprise their prey—usually other fishes.

Dorsal fin
Stomach
Kidney
Swim bladder
Spleen
Esophagus
Brain
Spinal cord inside backbone
Gill arch
Two-lobed caudal fin
Urine bladder
Heart
Anal fin
Vent (anus)
Right pectoral fin
Ovary (female)
Intestine
Liver
Right pelvic fin
Pyloric pouches

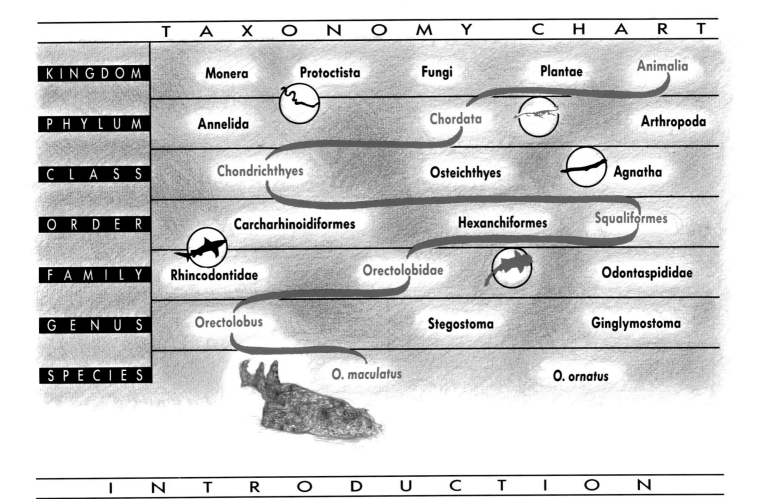

| | | | | | |
|---|---|---|---|---|---|
| **KINGDOM** | Monera | Protoctista | Fungi | Plantae | Animalia |
| **PHYLUM** | | Annelida | Chordata | | Arthropoda |
| **CLASS** | | Chondrichthyes | Osteichthyes | Agnatha | |
| **ORDER** | | Carcharhinoidiformes | Hexanchiformes | Squaliformes | |
| **FAMILY** | | Rhincodontidae | Orectolobidae | | Odontaspididae |
| **GENUS** | | Orectolobus | Stegostoma | Ginglymostoma | |
| **SPECIES** | | O. maculatus | | O. ornatus | |

# I N T R O D U C T I O N

Fishes! They fly, they walk, and, of course, they swim. This adaptable, varied group of animals has some common traits: all fishes have a backbone, or notocord, and an internal skeleton instead of an outer shell. They are ectothermic animals, which means they depend on the outside environment for body heat. (Mammals, in contrast, maintain a steady internal temperature.) Most fishes live in salt *or* fresh water (although some species spend parts of their lives in both). And fishes usually have scales and fins and breathe with their gills.

When it comes to habitat, fishes thrive on variety! Some species swim in icy, mountain streams, some cruise the deepest oceans, and some are restricted to a single desert pond.

There are about 20,000 species of fishes worldwide. They can be divided into three main groups: jawless fishes, cartilaginous fishes, and bony fishes. Lampreys and hagfishes are jawless. Sharks, rays, and skates are cartilaginous (their skeletons are made of cartilage instead of bone). Lungfishes, carp, groupers, and thousands of other species are bony fishes.

Scientists use a universal system of classification called taxonomy to keep track of fishes and the millions of animal and plant species on earth. Taxonomy begins with the five main groups of all living things, the kingdoms, and then divides those into the next group down, phylum, then class, order, family, genus, and finally, species. Members of a *species* look similar, and they can reproduce with each other.

For an example of how taxonomy works, follow the highlighted lines above to see how the spotted wobbegong Australian carpet shark is classified. In this book, the scientific name of each fish is given next to the common name. The first word is the genus; the second word is the species. In the case of the spiny-tooth parrotfish, the family name is given.

Turn to the *glossarized index* at the back of this book if you're looking for a specific fish, or for special information (what's a bony fish, for instance), or for a word you don't understand.

# Beaky Smile!

### Spiny-tooth Parrot Fish (Family: Scaridae)

MARY SUNDSTROM

Complete with a very toothy beak, colorful parrot fishes are well equipped to scrape algae from coral reefs in tropical seas around the world. Parrot fishes are herbivores (animal who feed only on plants), but they often take bites of coral along with algae. They use toothlike plates in the back of their throat to crush and grind each tough mouthful. They digest what's usable and expel the rest, and their droppings create calcified piles of white coral sand.

Parrot fishes are steady swimmers, and their caudal (tail) fin is made for cruising (it even works for a quick getaway from predators). Although they do not usually travel in schools, they are sometimes called "cattle of the sea." That's because parrot fishes have a strong homing instinct, and groups can be seen heading toward special feeding grounds as the tides go in or out.

Some parrot fishes have an unusual sleeping habit. As night falls, the fish begins to secrete a thick mucous that surrounds its body like a sleeping bag. The process takes about thirty minutes to complete. The mucous sac helps protect the parrot fish from nocturnal (nighttime) predators like the moray eel. In the morning, the fish struggles to emerge from its sac (this also takes about 30 minutes) and begins its search for food.

There are more than 75 species of parrot fishes, all of them colorful. Parrot fishes of some species change colors two or more times as they mature in a lifetime, and males and females may or may not be the same color. The spiny-tooth parrot fish is not as beaky as its relatives. True to its name, it's toothy!

School's out! Many species of fishes swim together in groups called schools. Fishes may school together to breed, to feed, or for safety in numbers because predators find large schools confusing. Ichthyologists have learned that schooling fishes use body coloring and water vibrations to stay together with their neighbors.

Parrot fishes use their beaky teeth to bite off chunks of coral reef with each mouthful of algae. Coral looks like a rock, right? Actually, it is made of skeletons! There's nothing spooky about it because the skeletons belonged to microscopic sea creatures.

In the sink! Swim bladders keep many fishes from sinking to the bottom even though they are heavier than seawater. This gas-filled chamber allows a fish to increase its volume without adding to its weight. A fish deflates its bladder to lower its body and inflates it to rise.

MARY LAMBERT

Photo, facing page, courtesy Scott Johnson/Photo Researchers, Inc.

F I S H E S

Out of more than 20,000 fish species worldwide, only about 50 are poisonous. Stingrays, stonefishes, and lionfishes are among those that can cause painful problems for humans. But poisonous fishes mostly use their venom as a defense against large fish predators.

## Stonefish (*Synanceia verrucosa*)

The warty, blobby, blotchy stonefish can be deadly. In fact, it has the most poisonous venom of all fishes! The spines of its dorsal fin (located on its back) are as sharp as hypodermic needles, and they are made for injecting poison. Skin divers must be especially careful because a stonefish is hard to spot. All those warts and blobs on the fish's skin provide camouflage; waiting for unsuspecting prey to swim by, a stonefish looks much like a rock or stone on the ocean bottom. If an unlucky swimmer steps on a stonefish, the pressure of his body weight will cause venom glands (located near the base of the dorsal fin spines) to inject poison into his foot. Stonefish poison has been known to kill a human within two hours of injection!

There are ten species of stonefish; most live in tropical seas where they prefer rocky bottom areas. This particular stonefish lives in Indo-Pacific waters. Some ichthyologists (ick-thee-OL-oh-gists), scientists who study fishes, believe stonefishes are related to scorpionfishes, while other scientists group stonefishes in their very own family: Synanceiidae.

Fishy feelies! Landlubbers have nothing to compare with a fish's lateral line. These sensory receptors lining the body of many fishes detect any change in surrounding water pressure, direction, or flow, as well as low-frequency sound.

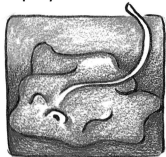

Stingrays—named for the poisonous sting of their whip-thin tail—may weigh more than 500 pounds (almost 300 kg) and have a wingspan greater than 10 feet (3 m). These giants hang out on sandy ocean bottoms and cruise in search of crustaceans and fishes to eat.

Photo, facing page, courtesy Steinhart Aquarium/Photo Researchers, Inc.

# FISHES

## Blackdevil Deep Sea Angler (*Melanocetus johnsonii*)

In the dark depths of the sea, deep sea anglerfishes use a special angle to catch their food. They have built-in lures —the first spine of the dorsal fin is often tipped with a glowing fringe—to attract small fish and other prey. Because deep sea anglers usually live several thousand feet below the ocean's surface, the light-producing tip of the angler's lure glows in the dark.

Some species of anglerfishes live in shallow water where there is natural light. In these circumstances, other fishes can see their lure without the attraction of special light-producing chemicals.

Of the eleven or so species of deep sea anglers, the blackdevil, which lives in the North Atlantic Ocean, does indeed look devilish. Its gaping, hungry mouth and long, sharp teeth are fierce. But most prey see the inviting lure, not the hungry blackdevil angler. Deep sea anglers are not very swift swimmers; they depend on their lures to attract their prey to them.

Fishes of four families of deep sea anglers have a special relationship between the sexes. At a very early age, the male angler becomes a parasite to the female. He may be only as big as the female's eye, and he attaches his mouth to her body—permanently!—so that they become one body. They even share circulation. When the female is ready to lay her eggs, she doesn't have to worry about finding a mate to fertilize them. She's already got a built-in sperm-producing appendage.

Finny fin fin! Fins are handy, and leggy, too, because fishes depend on their fins the way humans depend on arms and legs. Most fishes have two types of fins: median fins, which are along the animal's midline, and paired fins (one on each side).

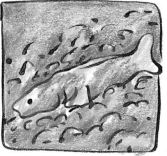

Anglerfishes use camouflage to entice prey to their built-in lures. Other fishes use camouflage to hide from larger predators. Body shape, color, schooling patterns, and swimming styles are some of the ways fishes blend in with their surroundings.

Dorsal fins (some fishes have up to three), the caudal (tail) fin, and the anal (or ventral) fin are all median fins. Dorsal and anal fins keep fishes stable, while the caudal fin provides forward thrust. The pectoral fins and pelvic fins are paired (they are the equivalent of human arms and bird wings), and they help with steering.

Photo, facing page, courtesy Peter David/Photo Researchers, Inc.

F I S H E S

# A Pop-eyed Hop and a Skip!

## Mudskipper (*Periophthalmus barbarus*)

At low tide among the mangroves in the muddy swamps of Africa, Southeast Asia, and Australasia, you'll find mudskippers hopping and "skipping" about like frogs—out of water! Their bulging eyes rise like mini headlamps from their large heads, giving them an even froggier look. Pectoral fins act as legs while long fishy tails trail behind. They can move so quickly that icthyologists are left in the mud. Mudskippers spend most of their air time searching for insects to eat, or they might be on the lookout for a mate or even chasing away other mudskippers.

Since a mudskipper is a fish, how does it breathe air? Easily, because it is equipped with an aqualung of sorts, which is actually water caught inside its gill chambers. For extra breathing power, it also absorbs oxygen through the skin of its throat and mouth.

Mudskippers aren't the only fishes that can breathe air. Three hundred-million-year-old lungfishes have both gills *and* lungs. They can gulp air into their mouths! Some lungfishes bury themselves in the earth during times of drought and wait for rain.

Mudskippers belong to a group of fishes called gobies. Of about 2,000 species of gobies, only a few can spend time out of water and survive.

Stranded at low tide, some water-only fishes use their pectoral (chest) fins to push themselves off bare rocks and back into the ocean.

When they are on land, mudskippers keep their pop-eyes wet by rolling them around in their sockets! Their eyes are also covered with a clear layer of very thick skin.

Speedy slime! The scales of most fishes are slimy for two reasons: slime is a lubricant, which makes it easier for a fish to move through water with less friction; slime seals a fish and makes it watertight. Without slime, ocean fish would soak up so much salt from the sea they would be poisoned.

Photo, facing page, courtesy Zig Leszczynski/Photo Researchers, Inc.

# Going Batty

## Longnosed Batfish (*Ogcocephalus vespertilio*)

Swimming clumsily and rolling across the sea bottom like a tank on leglike and armlike fins, the comical batfish doesn't look anything like an agile bat in motion! Batfishes are named for their large pectoral fins or "bat wings," not for their graceful moves.

When it comes to fishing, the batfish has a special line tucked inside the thin tube located just above its mouth. During fishing forays, the rod pushes out of the tube and rotates so the lumpy wormlike lure at the tip's end vibrates temptingly to attract hungry fish. Burrowed into the sand, the batfish lies in wait; when prey swims close enough, the batfish shoots out of hiding and gulps it down.

Batfishes are sandy-bottom dwellers of mostly deep but sometimes shallow warm seas all over the world. They are poor swimmers and often prefer "walking" using their sturdy pelvic fins for bottom navigation.

The longnosed batfish lives in warm Caribbean and Atlantic waters. It is 10 inches long at most, and its lumpy, warty body provides camouflage in sandy bottoms.

When is a fish not a fish? Well, shellfish—cuttlefish and mussels, for instance—are mollusks. Crayfish and starfish are not fishes, either! They just have fishy names.

Are you a fish? Pisces is the zodiac sign for fish. If you were born between February 19 and March 20, you are a bit fishy.

Salmon live in the sea, right? Well, sometimes. But they swim and leap up rivers to spawn in freshwater. They are *anadromous*! Eels do it vice versa, so call them *catadromous*.

Photo, facing page, courtesy Mike Neumann/Photo Researchers, Inc.

## Panamic Green Moray (*Gymnothorax castaneus*)

Razor-sharp teeth in a gaping mouth, leathery skin that is scaleless and wrinkled, and a long snakelike body make the Panamic green moray a fish you want to avoid. These fishes prefer to lurk in rocky caves and coral crevices waiting for fish and other prey to swim by (sometimes at night they'll slither into deep water in search of food). All it takes is a forward thrust of the head, a snap of the jaw, and the satisfied moray coils back into its lair to wait for more food.

Although morays are fierce predators, they don't scare everybody. Some species of shrimp work as moray "cleaners." They crawl all around the moray's head (they even climb inside its toothy mouth!) removing parasites and scraps of food, and the moray never harms them.

Green morays get their name from the yellow slime covering their blue body: the result is a weird brownish-green color. Most green morays are less than 5 feet long, but a few reach a length of 10 feet!

The Panamic green moray lives in warm waters of North and South America. There are more than 110 species of morays, including the zebra, the spotted, and the dragon, living in tropical and subtropical waters. Morays are known for a sharp sense of smell (the better to sniff food) and a short temper when provoked. Skin divers have died from infection after receiving a deep, poisonous bite from an irritated moray. But morays attack only when threatened, and most of the time, they would rather hide than fight.

**Big mouth!** Some species of morays have such big mouths they can't close them.

For Ancient Romans, a pool filled with moray eels was a sign of wealth and good eats.

**Mythical beast?** Oarfishes are long snakelike fishes that resemble true eels. They reach a length of more than 10 feet (and according to unauthenticated reports, 20 feet!) and cruise the oceans. Oarfishes may be the mythical sea creatures that sailors have told of for centuries.

"Elvers" are baby eels, not elves.

Photo, facing page, courtesy Mike Neumann/Photo Researchers, Inc.

# FISHES

# Pregnant Pops!

### Australian Sea Horse (*Hippocampus breviceps*)

When does a Pop become a Mom? When he's a sea horse, of course. Male sea horses really do become pregnant! But first, they must meet females and play the mating game.

Courtship begins at dawn, and it is colorful. Both males and females display bright colors—pinks and oranges—to let others know they're available. The male also fills his special abdominal pouch with water. When a pair meets, they wrap their prehensile (grasping) tails around a comfortable holdfast and begin to circle like horses on a carousel.

Soon, the male is ready to receive the female's eggs. In preparation, he begins to jacknife his body while pumping water in and out of his pouch (the same movement the male will use later to release young sea horses at birth). This is the signal for the female to place her ovipositor (egg-laying tube) inside the opening of the male's pouch. There, the eggs are fertilized by his sperm, and the female's job is finished. It is up to Pop to protect, care for, and nourish the developing embryos for the next few weeks until birth. Labor can take a few hours or even days.

Sea horses are special in other ways, too. Each of their two eyes work independently—all the better to spy small crustaceans and other prey to ambush. A quick, strong, suck of the sea horse's snout disposes of a meal, which they digest without the help of teeth or stomach. How? Even icthyologists aren't sure!

Sea horses move with the help of their single dorsal fin, and they also have two teensy pectoral fins for steering and balance. They are the world's slooowwwest fish, moving less than one foot per minute. That speed wouldn't win any horse races!

There are about 35 species of sea horses living in shallow coastal seas all the way from Tasmania in the south to the English Channel in the north. They range in length from the half-inch New Caledonian sea horse to the 14-inch Eastern Pacific sea horse. This fish family also includes seadragons and pipefishes.

What fish has a horse's head, a monkey's tail, and a pouch like a kangaroo? A male sea horse, of course!

How do we know the pregnant "Pop" isn't really a "Mom"? Icthyologists have proven that male sea horses produce sperm like all male animals, and females produce eggs.

Ancient Romans believed sea horses could help cure baldness when their ashes were applied to the head. These days, we know you would have better luck with a toupee!

Photo, facing page, courtesy Paul A. Zahl/Photo Researchers, Inc.

# F I S H E S

### Burrfish (*Chilomycterus schoepfi*)

It looks more like a balloon, or a paper sculpture, than a fish! Actually, it is a burrfish in its larval (pre-adult) stage. Many animals go through larval stages—when they look different from their parents—before they become fully mature.

The burrfish is a very close relative of the porcupine fish, but it's a different sort of critter. A porcupine fish will raise its spines and inflate its body with air or water (like a balloon) when it wants to discourage predators. A burrfish, in contrast, is always swimming around with semi-raised spines. Either way, bigger is scarier—and also too much of a mouthful for many predatory fishes.

Fishes aren't the only animals who try to make themselves look fierce. Threat behavior is part of life for many animals. Frogs, lizards, monkeys, and even humans try to look bigger than they really are to avoid dangerous encounters.

There are about 16 species of porcupine fish and burrfish swimming in the tropical ocean waters of the world.

**The barbel to feel you with!** Barbels are whiskery growths on the snouts of some fishes, and they contain sensory receptors for taste (or smell) and touch.

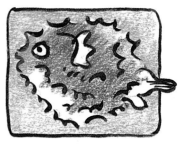

**Pufferfish puff up sideways, not longways!** The length of a pufferfish stays the same when it inflates its body, while the width expands like a balloon.

Photo, facing page, courtesy Kjell B. Sandved/Photo Researchers, Inc.

# FISHES

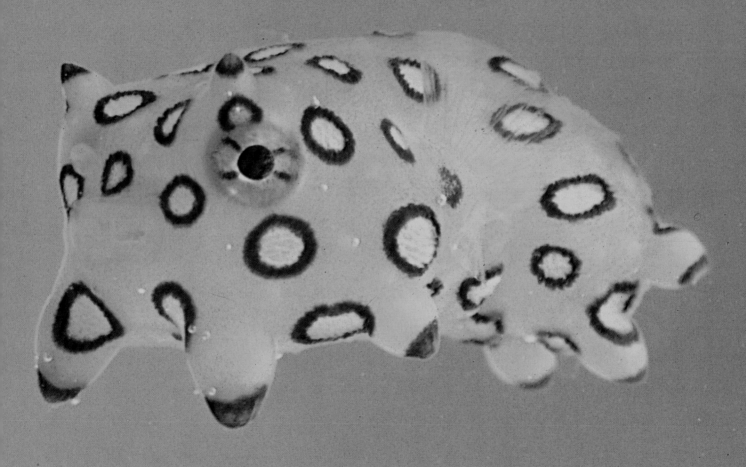

# Bubble Double

### Bubble-eye Goldfish (*Carassius auratus*)

Not all goldfish are gold! In fact, some have red caps and pink eyes, others sport black, red, and white spots, and there are even silvery black-scaled goldfish. How did they get that way?

According to Chinese legend, there was a great drought almost 3,000 years ago (769 B.C.) when no rain fell for 100 days. To appease the gods, the farmers made sacrificial gifts to the dry ponds, and, suddenly, a burbling brook splashed out of the ground—filled with tiny gold fishes! And at just that very moment, the rains began to fall.

Even if the legend isn't true, for centuries, people in Asia have been raising goldfishes. In about 960, a Chinese governor of the Sung dynasty created a beautiful goldfish pond, and there was once a harsh penalty for anyone who tried to kill and eat the fish for food. By 1136, there were historical reports that people were breeding goldfishes artificially, some of which turned into extremely, extremely weird fishes!

Goldfishes, carp, and minnows all belong to the same family. Wild goldfishes (a.k.a. Johnny carp, Missouri minnow, and crucian carp) are a dull brown color and a basic fish shape. They are also the ancestors of all exotic goldfishes! Only after breeders begin pairing and mating fishes with special qualities do exotic breeds like the bubble-eye goldfish appear! If exotic goldfishes are allowed to breed naturally, their offspring eventually regain the plain-John look of a Johnny carp.

Tiny or tall? Goldfish grow as large as their surroundings allow. In a small aquarium, they will enlarge just a few inches, but placed in a pond, they begin to grow and grow and grow—sometimes as much as 18 inches!

A healthy goldfish can live for twenty years when it is well cared for!

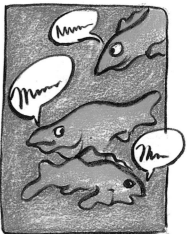

Goldfish have good hearing and often "murmur" among themselves, and they can easily be trained to respond to the sound of a bell.

Photo, facing page, courtesy Tom McHugh/Photo Researchers, Inc.

## Spotted Wobbegong Australian Carpet Shark (*Orectolobus maculatus*)

Jaws! Sharks are fierce predators with teeth as sharp as razors and jaws as strong as steel traps, right? Aggressive tiger sharks, great white (or man-eater) sharks, and hammerheads might holler a hearty "Aye, aye," but other sharks would tell a different story. For instance, the 40-foot whale shark dines only on tiny fish and plankton (microscopic organisms), the snakelike frill shark prefers squid, and the bottom-dwelling carpet shark just waits for crabs and fishes to pass by.

All 250 or so species of sharks do have *some* things in common. They (and their relatives, rays and skates) are known for their well-developed lower jaws and bony teeth as well as their skeletons, which are made of cartilage instead of bone. The cartilage is hard, not rubbery, and that is one reason many sharks have such powerful bites. Sharks have several rows of teeth and two nostrils that do not open into their mouth. Their scales are toothlike in structure. And, of course, they have dorsal fins! They are mostly marine fish, although a few species will travel up freshwater rivers.

The spotted wobbegong is a carpet shark that lives off the coast of Australia and other tropical Indonesian and Pacific waters. It is a carnivore (flesh-eater) and prefers small fish and crabs. Like all sharks, it is extra-weird looking! It boasts a broad snout fringed with feathery, weedy-looking barbels. Its bumpy brownish body is mottled with lots of eyespots (spots that look like eyes), which provide camouflage and a rocklike appearance on the ocean floor.

The "yikes" bite! Sharks have many rows of teeth, and the outer ones are always replaced by inner ones.

Size it up. The world's largest fish, the whale shark, reaches a length of almost 50 feet (about 15 m) and weighs in at 20 tons! The teensiest fish is the 0.3-inch-long (8 mm) dwarf pygmy goby.

Speedy ocean swimmers such as sharks, tuna, and rays have no swim bladder. These fish will sink slowly whenever they stop swimming. For this reason, they are *always* on the move.

FISHES

### Spotfin Jawfish (*Opistognathus macrognathus*)

It's no surprise that a fish known as the jawfish has a big head and plenty of jawbone. In fact, the spotfin jawfish can open its mouth wide enough to eat a fish that is larger than its own head! But jawfishes use their mouths for other purposes.

Some male jawfishes incubate their young by the mouthful. Eggs are carried orally until the young hatch and are ready to swim on their own. Even then, the fry (young fishes) stay very close to their parents and swim for cover (sometimes inside their parent's mouth) whenever danger threatens.

Although jawfishes look fierce, they only reach a length of 6 inches or less. For safety and shelter, some species make holes in the sand and adorn the entrance with pebbles, shells, and bits of coral. They enter tail first at the first sign of danger and peer out to see if all is clear.

Jawfishes swim in the warm waters of the Atlantic Ocean, the Gulf of Mexico, the Caribbean, the Indian Ocean, and the Gulf of California region.

A mouthful! This male jawfish has a mouth filled with eggs. It is his job to incubate the eggs until they hatch.

When it comes to reproduction, fishes are a varied group. Many species release their eggs into water where they are fertilized and develop on their own. Others, like the jawfish, incubate eggs in their mouth. Still others, sharks, for instance, give birth to live young. Skates and rays, in contrast, lay already fertilized eggs inside egg cases (sometimes known as a ''mermaid's purse'') that attach to seaweed.

Photo, facing page, courtesy Fred McConnaughey/Photo Researchers, Inc.

Photo, facing page, courtesy Steinhart Aquarium/Photo Researchers, Inc.

Breathing easy! Primitive fishes (those most like their fish ancestors) have two ways to breathe—through gills *and* lungs.

## Pacific Hagfish (*Eptatretus stouti*)

Wormy and *extremely* slimy, Pacific hagfishes are the ugliest of the uglies! Hags are also the most primitive of all fishes, which means they are simplest in structure. They are jawless fishes, eellike in shape, with a skeleton made of cartilage instead of bone. Their skin is scaleless as well as slippery. When they are distressed, hags secrete lots of slime from mucous glands in their reddish, gray-brown skin. They have one nostril (which they use to find prey), but their eyes are not visible, and they're blind.

Hagfishes are scavengers and spend their lives imbedded in soft muddy ocean bottoms where the water is cold and deep. Only their snouts can be seen. They emerge after dark to feed on dead or injured fishes—how hags eat is even weirder than how they look—from the *inside out*. They penetrate the skin of another fish by boring a hole with their raspy tongue. Once they have a grip with their triangular lips, they eat out the intestines first and then the flesh, leaving only skin and bones.

Pacific hagfishes live off the coast of North America. Other species of hagfish live in almost all parts of the world—in the North Atlantic Ocean, the Mediterranean Sea, the Sea of Japan, and off the coasts of South Africa and South America.

Why don't bony fish roll over? Deep bodies, much like a sailboat's keel, and dorsal fins keep bony fishes from keeling over.

Hagfishes grow to a length of two extremely weird feet.

F I S H E S

### Walking Catfish (*Clarias batrachus*)

Walking catfishes can walk about on land using their pectoral leglike fins and moving with a snakelike slither. Of course, that's not all it takes for these fishes to walk on land!

Walking catfishes have an extra-special lunglike breathing apparatus tucked in front of their gills and reaching along both sides of the spine like many roots well supplied with blood. This makes it possible for them to breathe air and stay out of water on rainy nights for as long as several hours. To make room for these extra "lungs," the front of their body is thick. Walking catfishes have a thin, flat tail, and their skin is covered with mucous for protection from the dry air.

These fishes grow to a length of 16 inches, and they are hardy. That hardiness has proved a problem for other fishes. Walking catfishes are native to Southeast Asia, but they have been imported by fish hobbyists to Guam, the Hawaiian Islands, and Florida where they were set free, escaped, or just walked away. Now they are thriving in their new homes, and they are threatening native species. Walking catfishes are extremely aggressive and will attack and eat almost any other fish—even if it's bigger than they are!

When they are in the swim, walking catfishes prefer slow-moving, dirty water. If the pond or their food supply dries up, they simply walk to new territory.

Pleased to meet you, now move over, buster! Just like walking catfish, many other plant and animal species have caused problems for native wildlife when they were introduced by humans. The wild dingo in Australia killed many animals that were there long before it arrived. Rats (brought by sailors) destroyed much of the tortoise population of the Galápagos Islands. And house cats are deadly predators of song birds and other wildlife in the United States and Europe.

Photo, facing page, courtesy Photo Researchers, Inc.

# FISHES

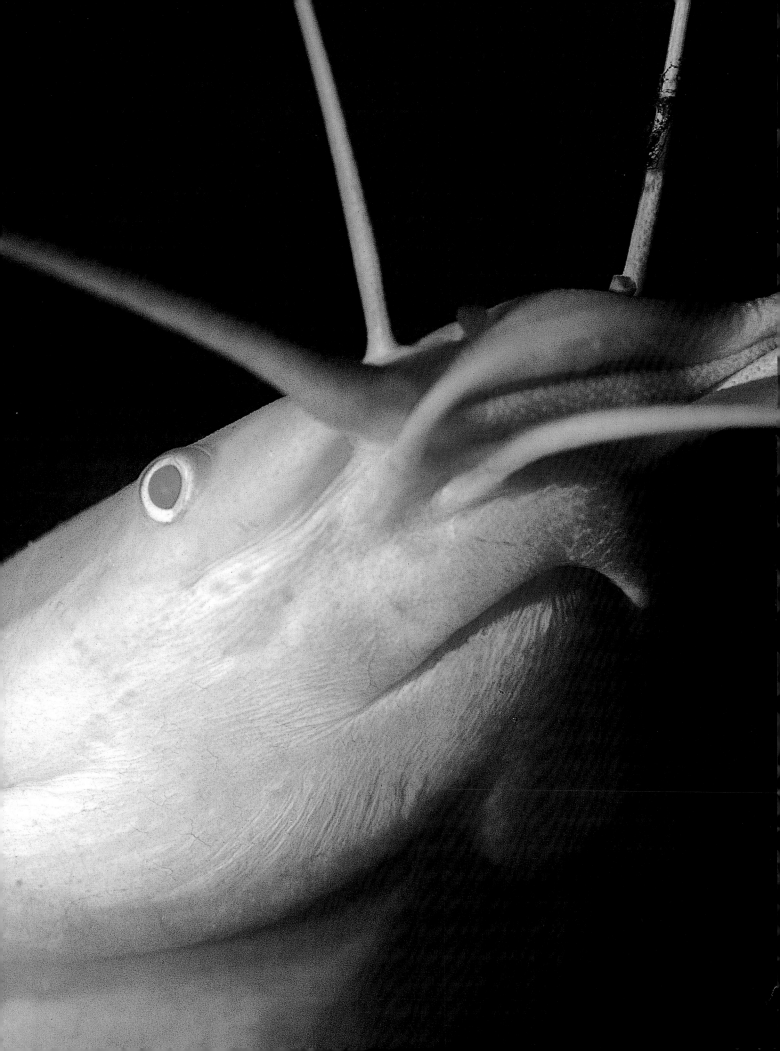

## C-O Sole (*Pleuronichthys coenosis*)

There are more than 500 species of flatfish—fishes that swim flat against the bottom of the sea. But how did they get that way? They weren't born flat!

Newly hatched flatfishes look like most larval fishes: they're small, and they swim upright. But just weeks later, drastic changes take place. Their bodies become flatter and flatter, and the eye on one side of their head slowly moves over the top to join the other eye. The blind side is now the downside, and the side with two eyes is on top. To make appearances even odder, the skull and the mouth also twist upward. Finally, flatfishes sink to the ocean bottom, where they stay for the rest of their very flat lives.

Depending on which side the eyes settle, flatfishes are known as "left-eyed" or "right-eyed." Members of the scientific family Bothidae—various flounders, sole, whiffs, halibuts, and sanddabs—are left-eyed. In contrast, members of the scientific family Pleuronectidae—some flounders, turbots, sole, and plaice—are right-eyed. The C-O sole, a right-eyed flounder, prefers warm seas worldwide.

Brazilian hiccup fish gulp air that sounds like a hiccup when released. The loudest hiccups can be heard as far away as a mile!

Turn signals. Fishes use their fins for balance, propulsion, braking, and steering. This fish looks as if it's about to make a right turn, but actually, it uses the right fin to turn to the left.

Small fry! Newly hatched fish are known as "fry."

FISHES

# Spit It Out!

## Red Devil Cichlid (*Cichlasoma labiatum*)

Splashy, rainbow-colored cichlids (like the red devil) live in tropical freshwater streams and lakes of North, Central, and South America, as well as Africa and India. A few robust species survive in salty or coastal areas. There are about 600 species in all.

Cichlids are aggressive carnivores that eat the flesh of other fish *and* small animals. But cichlid parents are attentive and careful: both males and females provide care and schooling for their offspring. While young cichlids are still under the watchful eye of grown-ups, they must stay in school, which means they stay together. If a single young cichlid tries to swim solo, a parent may grasp it by mouth and spit it back into the group.

Some species of cichlids are mouthbrooders, which means the female carries the eggs in her mouth. After the eggs hatch, the larvae remain in their mother's mouth for several days until they can swim on their own. Even then, they return to Mom when danger threatens. Cichlid species who are not mouthbrooders deposit their eggs on water plants, stones, and pieces of wood. When the young are newly hatched, their parents move them into a "nursery" dug in the sandy river or lake bottom.

Some mouthbrooding parents blow or spit their fry from their mouth when they are ready to feed. That way, the young can learn to feed, too. Fry return to the mouth when danger threatens or night falls.

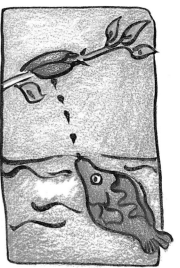

Another fish with spit is the archer fish of India and Australasia. This swamp-dwelling creature takes aim and squirts a stream of water above the water's surface to hit spiders and insects as far away as five feet (1.5 m).

Photo, facing page, courtesy Steinhart Aquarium/Photo Researchers, Inc.

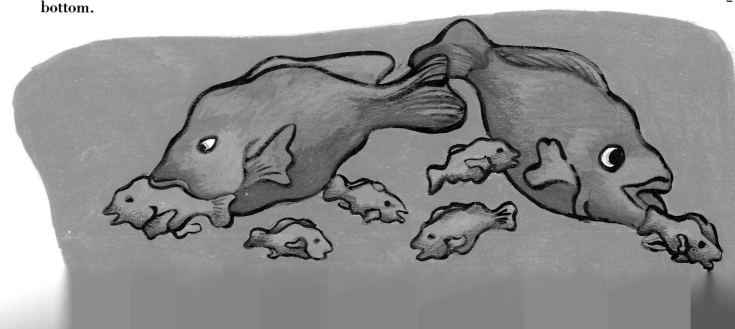

# Z-Z-Z-Z-Zap!

The electric eel of the Amazon uses electroplates in its muscles to deliver 500-volt shocks that can kill small prey.

## Elephant-nosed Fish (*Gnathonemus numenius*)

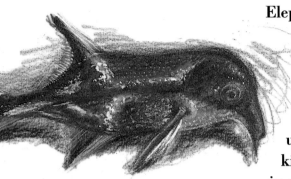

Elephant-nosed fish are shocking! At least, like many species of fish, their bodies produce electrical currents. Some fish, electric eels and electric catfishes, for instance, use their shocks to stun and kill prey. Elephant-nosed fish, in contrast, use their mild electrical abilities as a sort of radar to track food. Electrical currents are produced by specially modified muscles on both sides of the tail.

The elephant-nosed fish has a snout to shout about, but this snout is really a mouth! It is used to probe for food on muddy bottoms of African rivers, streams, and lakes where they live. Because an elephant-nosed fish has such a small mouth and very few teeth, it dines on small aquatic invertebrates such as insects, various larvae, and worms.

There are more than 100 species of these fish, and they all have a miniature elephant-sized mouth. They vary in length from 6 inches to 5 feet. They are active at night and hide from daylight.

Electric catfish deliver 100 volts of electricity. That's enough to stun and kill small fish. They also use it as underwater sonar to locate prey. Electric organs in the catfish are located in glandular cells in the skin instead of muscles.

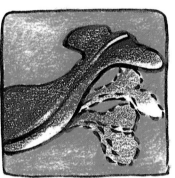

Nothing fishy! Whales, dolphins, and porpoises are marine mammals, not fishes. Their tails (flukes) are horizontal and move up and down. Fishes, in contrast, have vertical tail (caudal) fins that move side to side.

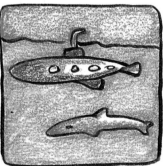

Submarines are designed to copy a fish's cylindrical body. They are tapered at the ends, and broad sides mimic the pectoral fins of fishes.

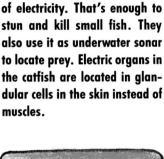

### Atlantic Wolf Fish (*Anarhichas lupas*)

Scaleless and snakelike in body shape, the Atlantic wolf fish may grow to a length of 5 feet and weigh as much as 30 pounds. Its reddish-brown body is striped with black and adorned with a long dorsal fin. It swims in the waters of the Atlantic Ocean off the American coasts as well as European coasts and the North Sea.

Atlantic wolf fishes use their great, toothy jaws to crush and crunch crustaceans and mollusks (including hard-shelled mussels, sea urchins, and starfishes). Shells and all are swallowed.

All nine species of wolf fishes (including wolf eels) are aggressive. Some species are fished commercially in North American and European waters where they are called catfishes. They have been known to bite through wood planks and hard leather boots after they've been caught.

Astronauts underwater! Fishes and water are almost the same density, so fishes are living in a weightless world. Unlike humans, fishes don't need their skeletons to support their body weight, so their bones are often extra-light.

400-million-year-old-fishes! The coelacanth (SEAL-ah-kanth) is alive and swimming today, although scientists used to believe the species had become extinct 80 million years ago. In 1938, science rediscovered them in South Africa when a fisherman fished one from the sea. It seems local people hadn't realized they were catching fossils.

Photo, facing page, courtesy Tom McHugh/Photo Researchers, Inc.

# FISHES

### Grouper (*Epinephelus summana*)

Groupers are nonschooling sea basses. They are also carnivores, and they have the jaws to prove it! The 100 or so grouper species, which live in tropical seas, have sharp, grasping teeth that point inward. They use these to prey on other fishes and sea animals.

Groupers range in size from almost weightless to more than one thousand pounds! One of the largest species lives off the Australian reef and is reported to stalk swimmers the way a cat stalks a mouse. Some divers have been terrified by the aggressive rush of this great fish. A grouper charging into action has so much power, the first thrust of its tail produces a loud sonic boom! Although groupers have never been known to attack divers, their threat behavior is scary enough to keep some people out of the water.

Groupers swim in all warm seas and prefer to gather along rocky shores and deep-water reefs. Red and Nassau groupers are common in Caribbean and Florida waters. Red hind and rock hind groupers swim in the Atlantic Ocean. *Epinephelus summana* lives in Indonesian and Pacific waters.

**Clean routine!** Some small fishes, such as wrasses, work as "cleaners" picking bits of food and tiny parasites off the skin, gills, and fins (even inside the mouth!) of larger fishes like huge groupers. This tidy partnership benefits both parties, and "dirty" fishes sometimes line up for a wash.

**Greek to thee!** *Ichthys* is Greek for fish.

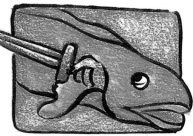

**A South Pacific legend tells us a great grouper once gulped a gorgeous girl because he loved her. The girl cut her way out of the grouper's body, and the wounds became gills. The grouper kept his gills but gave up on love.**

Photo, facing page, courtesy Rondi/Tandi/Photo Researchers, Inc.

Earth's first fishes appeared about 500 million years ago. Although they had backbones, they were jawless, finless, and scaleless—unlike most of their modern descendants. How do we know? Fish skeletons make good fossils because they were once made of bone.

Lampreys and hagfishes are the only jawless fishes living today. They feed solely by sucking or scraping their prey.

Visit a museum or a fossil store in your neighborhood. See if you are able to spot individual scales, fins, spines, and even eyes—all fossilized. Remember, these fishes were in the swim millions of years ago!

### Pacific Lamprey (*Lampetra tridentata*)

Like their relatives, the hagfishes, lampreys are jawless, eellike, and weirder than weird looking. But unlike marine hagfishes, lampreys spend their lives in fresh water, or, if they are marine species, they return to fresh water to spawn their eggs. And while hagfishes prey on dead or dying fish, some lampreys prey on the living.

Many lampreys are parasites; they attach themselves by mouth and teeth to a fish's skin and suck out blood and body fluids. The mouth glands of lampreys secrete anticoagulants—substances that keep the blood of their prey flowing. When they have sucked out all of a host's juices, they look for fresh prey.

Lampreys also use their mouths, or suckers, to anchor themselves to rocks, to carry stones to their nest, or for mating. During egg fertilization, the female attaches herself to a stone while the male attaches himself to the female—both using their suckers. Lamprey eggs hatch into burrowing larvae, and they remain in that life stage for 3 to 6 years before they mature. The change from larvae to adult may take 8 months, and during this time, lampreys cannot and do not feed. When the change is complete, parasitic lampreys begin to feed on the fluids of other fishes while nonparasitic lampreys simply breed and die.

There are about 24 species of lampreys found in temperate climates all over the world. Fourteen species live in the waters of North America, including the Great Lakes. The Pacific lamprey grows to a length of 27 inches. It is a marine species that thrives in the Pacific Ocean.

F I S H E S

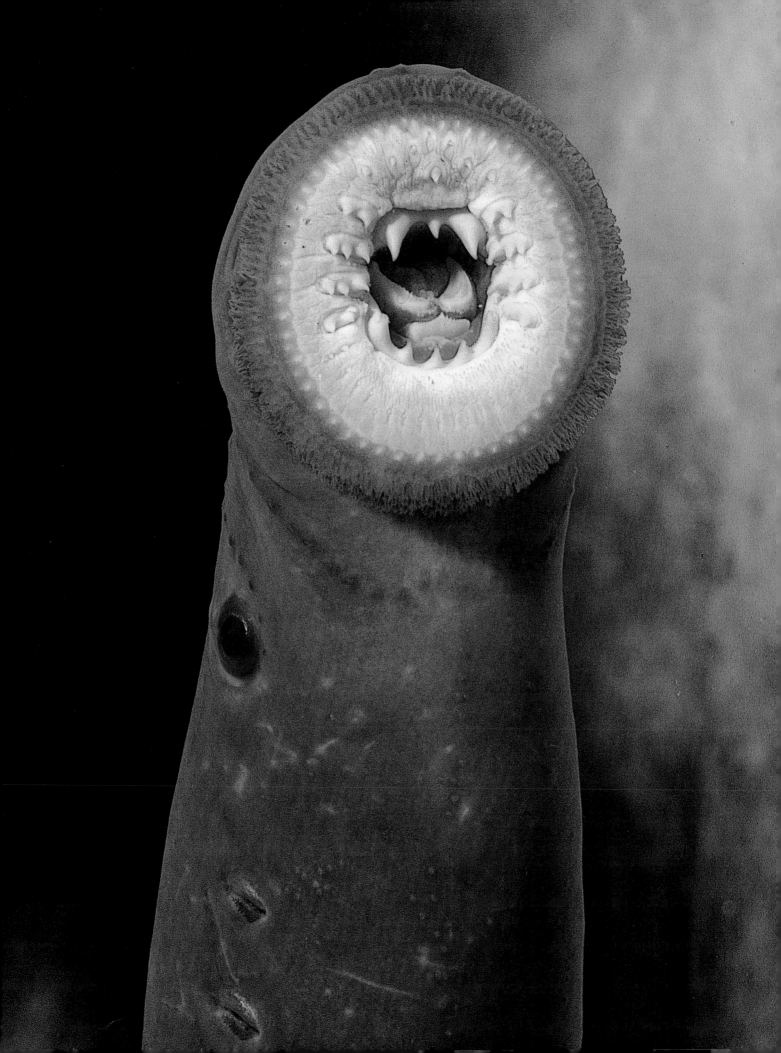

# Dragons of the Deep

From the horse's mouth! Ancient legend has it that sea horse and seadragon remains could cure leprosy, infertility, and rabies, but that's just a tall tale.

In many species of fishes, males are in charge of "child care." Male sea catfish carry eggs and fry by mouth, and male pipefish brood eggs.

## Leafy Seadragon (*Phyllopteryx eques*)

Is it a vine? A weed? An exotic plant from outer space? Actually, it is an extremely leafy seadragon camouflaged to look like the seaweed, algae, and eel grass common in the Australian coastal waters where it lives.

Like its relative, the sea horse, the male leafy seadragon is the one who cares for the eggs. He doesn't have a pouch (like the male sea horse). Instead, he packs the eggs below his tail where the skin becomes especially spongy. This happens before the male and female seadragons mate. After the female deposits her eggs underneath the male's tail, his skin hardens into a separate pouch for each egg. When the baby seadragons are ready to swim on their own, out they pop!

Like sea horses, leafy seadragons are not swift swimmers. Instead of speed, they depend on camouflage to avoid predators. Seadragons can change their reddish-brown color to match sea plants, and their leafy limbs sway in the ocean like weeds.

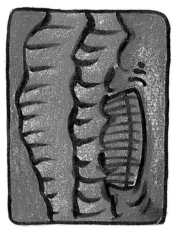

A sea horse uses the feathery fin on its back to travel. This fin vibrates as many as 70 times each second, and each vibration is a complete wave action that ripples top to bottom through the fin. A pair of pectoral fins behind the sea horse's head provides turning and steering power.

Photo, facing page, courtesy Paul A. Zahl/Photo Researchers, Inc.

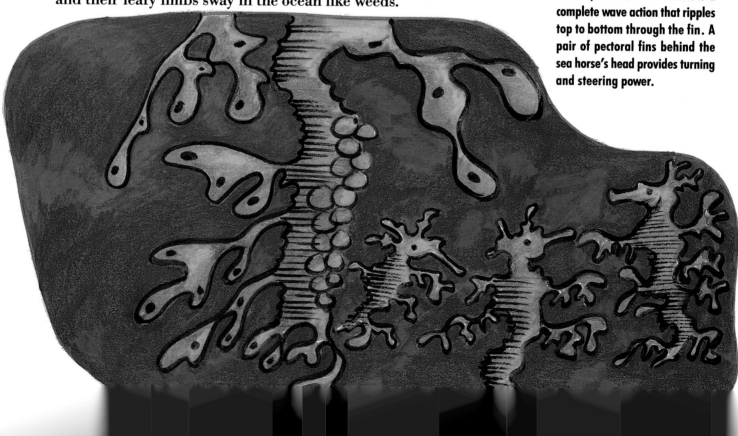

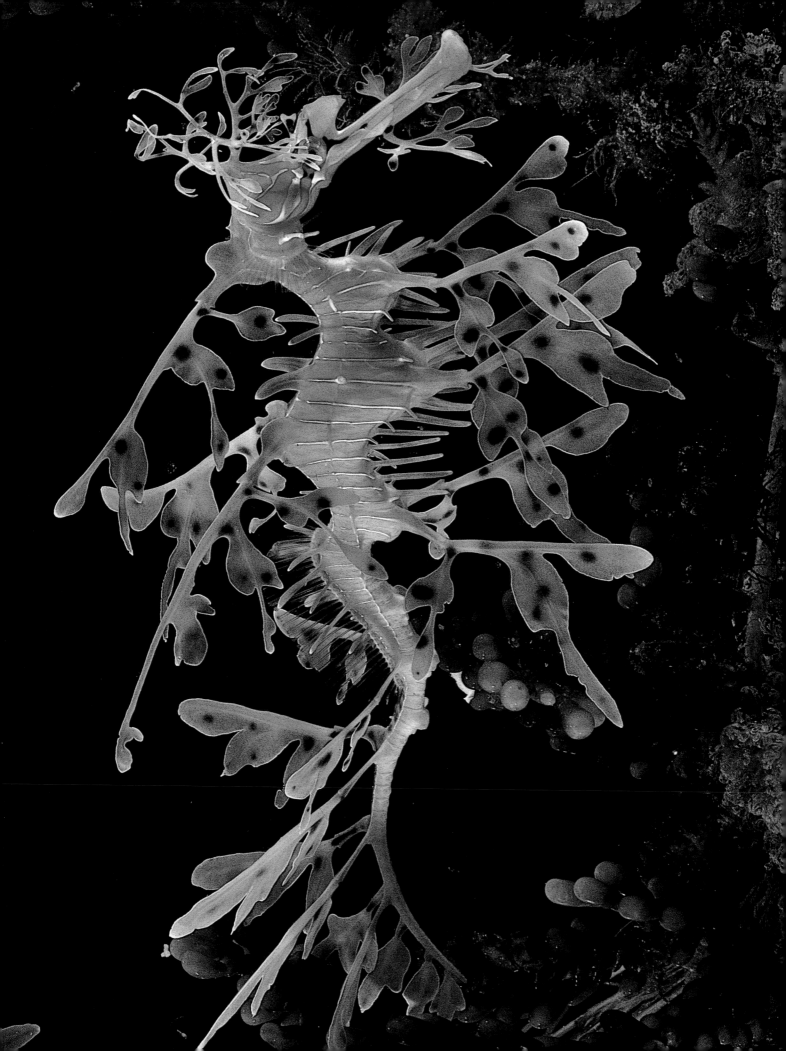

## Wolf-Eel (*Anarrhichthys ocellatus*)

The wolf-eel is no beauty king or queen, but it's a very important fish! This cold-water marine fish may grow 9 feet long, and its strong jaws are packed with sharp, broad teeth for grinding. Like its relative, the wolf fish, the wolf-eel thrives on crabs, starfish, sea urchins, and other very crunchy edibles. In fact, wolf-eels are important predators of sea urchins—they use their strong teeth to crush these spiny critters—and they help control urchin overpopulation! When wolf-eels are overhunted by humans, sea urchin populations grow unchecked and destroy the kelp beds where they thrive. Then, in a chain reaction, many sea creatures lose their kelp bed habitat. Just like on dry land, the balance of ocean life is a very delicate matter.

All nine species of wolf-eels, and their relatives, wolf fishes, live in cold oceans of Earth's Northern Hemisphere.

To drink or not to drink? Fishes who live in salty oceans drink lots of water because their bodies lose it. Freshwater fishes, in contrast, absorb water through the body so they must get rid of it through their urine.

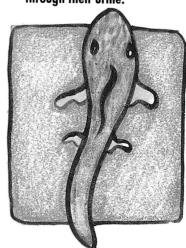

Wavy undulation is the usual method of movement underwater. Most aquatic animals make curve after curve with their body—head to tail—like a moving wave. Most fishes (like sea snakes) create waves in a horizontal plane, but flatfishes move in a vertical plane.

Fishes use their fins to paddle nowhere! When they want to hover in place, turn, dive, or stop, fins are the ticket.

Photo, facing page, courtesy Neil G. McDaniel/Photo Researchers, Inc.

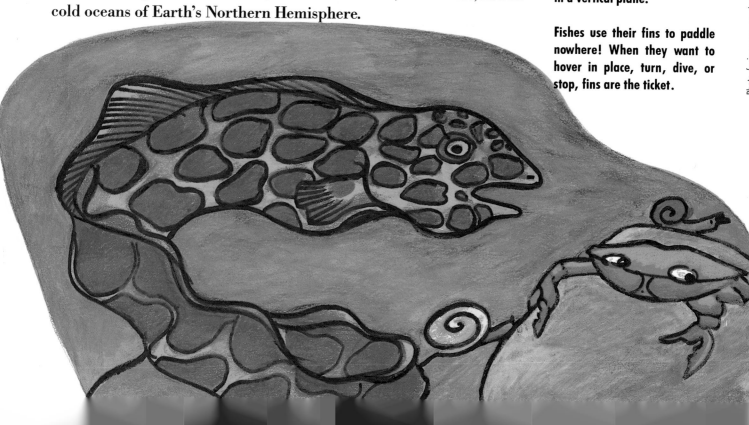

This glossarized index will help you find specific fish information. It will also help you understand the meaning of some of the words used in this book.

## EXTREMELY WEIRD SERIES

All of the titles are written by Sarah Lovett, 8¹/₂" x 11", 48 pages, $9.95 paperback, $14.95 hardcover, with color photographs and illustrations.

Extremely Weird Bats
Extremely Weird Birds
Extremely Weird Endangered Species
Extremely Weird Fishes
Extremely Weird Frogs
Extremely Weird Insects
Extremely Weird Mammals
Extremely Weird Micro Monsters
Extremely Weird Primates
Extremely Weird Reptiles
Extremely Weird Sea Creatures
Extremely Weird Snakes
Extremely Weird Spiders

## X-RAY VISION SERIES

Each title in the series is 8¹/₂" x 11", 48 pages, $9.95 paperback, with color photographs and illustrations, and written by Ron Schultz.

Looking Inside the Brain
Looking Inside Cartoon Animation
Looking Inside Caves and Caverns
Looking Inside Sports Aerodynamics
Looking Inside Sunken Treasure
Looking Inside Telescopes and the Night Sky

## THE KIDDING AROUND TRAVEL GUIDES

All of the titles listed below are 64 pages and $9.95 paperbacks, except for Kidding Around the National Parks and Kidding Around Spain, which are 108 pages and $12.95 paperbacks.

Kidding Around Atlanta
Kidding Around Boston, 2nd ed.
Kidding Around Chicago, 2nd ed.
Kidding Around the Hawaiian Islands
Kidding Around London
Kidding Around Los Angeles
Kidding Around the National Parks
  of the Southwest
Kidding Around New York City, 2nd ed.
Kidding Around Paris
Kidding Around Philadelphia
Kidding Around San Diego
Kidding Around San Francisco
Kidding Around Santa Fe
Kidding Around Seattle
Kidding Around Spain
Kidding Around Washington, D.C., 2nd ed.

## MASTERS OF MOTION SERIES

Each title in the series is 10¹/₄" x 9", 48 pages, $9.95 paperback, with color photographs and illustrations.

How to Drive an Indy Race Car
  David Rubel
How to Fly a 747
  Tim Paulson
How to Fly the Space Shuttle
  Russell Shorto

## THE KIDS EXPLORE SERIES

Each title is written by kids for kids by the Westridge Young Writers Workshop, 7" x 9", and $9.95 paperback, with photographs and illustrations by the kids.

Kids Explore America's Hispanic Heritage
112 pages
Kids Explore America's African American Heritage 128 pages
Kids Explore the Gifts of Children with Special Needs 128 pages
Kids Explore America's Japanese American Heritage 144 pages

## ENVIRONMENTAL TITLES

Habitats: *Where the Wild Things Live*
Randi Hacker and Jackie Kaufman
8¹/₂" x 11", 48 pages, color illustrations, $9.95 paper

The Indian Way: *Learning to Communicate with Mother Earth*
Gary McLain
7" x 9", 114 pages, two-color illustrations, $9.95 paper

Rads, Ergs, and Cheeseburgers: *The Kids' Guide to Energy and the Environment*
Bill Yanda
7" x 9", 108 pages, two-color illustrations, $13.95 paper

The Kids' Environment Book: *What's Awry and Why*
Anne Pedersen
7" x 9", 192 pages, two-color illustrations, $13.95 paper

## BIZARRE & BEAUTIFUL SERIES

*A* spirited and fun investigation of the mysteries of the five senses in the animal kingdom.

Each title in the series is 8½" x 11", $9.95 paperback, $14.95 hardcover, with color photographs and illustrations throughout.

**Bizarre & Beautiful Ears**
**Bizarre & Beautiful Eyes**
**Bizarre & Beautiful Feelers**
**Bizarre & Beautiful Noses**
**Bizarre & Beautiful Tongues**

## RAINBOW WARRIOR SERIES

*W* hat is a Rainbow Warrior Artist? It is a person who strives to live in harmony with the Earth and all living creatures, and who tries to better the world while living his or her life in a creative way.

Each title is written by Reavis Moore with a foreword by LeVar Burton, and is 8½" x 11", 48 pages, $14.95 hardcover, with color photographs and illustrations.

**Native Artists of Africa**
**Native Artists of North America**
**Native Artists of Europe**

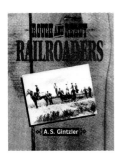

## ROUGH AND READY SERIES

*L* earn about the men and women who settled the American West. Explore the myths and legends about these courageous individuals and learn about the environmental, cultural, and economic legacies they left to us.

Each title in the series is written by A. S. Gintzler and is 48 pages, 8½" x 11", $12.95 hardcover, with two-color illustrations and duotone archival photographs.

**Rough and Ready Cowboys**
**Rough and Ready Homesteaders**
**Rough and Ready Loggers**

**Rough and Ready
 Outlaws & Lawmen**
**Rough and Ready Prospectors**
**Rough and Ready Railroaders**

## AMERICAN ORIGINS SERIES

*M* any of us are the third and fourth generation of our families to live in America. Learn what our great-great-grandparents experienced when they arrived here and how much of our lives are still intertwined with theirs.

Each title is 48 pages, 8½" x 11", $12.95 hardcover, with two-color illustrations and duotone archival photographs.

**Tracing Our English Roots**
**Tracing Our French Roots**
**Tracing Our German Roots**
**Tracing Our Irish Roots**

**Tracing Our Italian Roots**
**Tracing Our Japanese Roots**
**Tracing Our Jewish Roots**
**Tracing Our Polish Roots**

| For U.S. Orders Totaling | Add |
| --- | --- |
| Up to $15.00 | $4.25 |
| $15.01 to $45.00 | $5.25 |
| $45.01 to $75.00 | $6.25 |
| $75.01 or more | $7.25 |